faith

MV STEPHEN DAVIES
The Last Mission Ship
Part One

ISBN 978-0-6457776-1-1

Published by Uncharted Collective April 2023
Copyright Michael J Smith 2023
www.unchartedletters.com

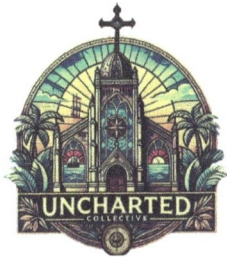

DEDICATION

To my best friend and lifelong mate and wife, Sonia Minniecon-Smith, and my other best friend, buddy and son William, who have had to put up with my "wooden boat disease" despite themselves having caught a slight case of it themselves.

And to the Ship itself, whose dedication to the people and communities of Cape York and the Torres Strait was with unquestioned service, and is worthy of the very reason for this book. May it lead to the Ship's revival.

And to my mum, whose uncanny saying for me was 'never give up', before we lost you when I was only a teen. The discipline and service you showed to those around you was also above and beyond in each and every way.

MV STEPHEN DAVIES

THE LAST
MISSION
SHIP

FROM THE PEN OF

MICHAEL J SMITH
Uncharted Collective

MV *Stephen Davies* is the last Missionary Ship built under sail for Australia's last frontier Missions, dotted throughout remote Cape York and the Torres Strait.

MV *Stephen Davies* may also well be the last sailing Missionary Ship surviving in the South Seas.

MV *Stephen Davies*' story, along with the many owners, missionaries, government officials, passengers and crew and their children who stepped aboard her, all have a story to tell, long into the next century.

MV *Stephen Davies* still has a role to play. We need your support to bring one of the last Mission vessels built under sail, back into service to do some of the good work that she was built for.

FOREWORD

The Last Mission Ship - Part One, has been produced on behalf of *Uncharted Collective* with the aim of raising awareness of what is believed to be the last Mission vessel built for sail in Australian and South Sea waters - the seventy-two year old MV *Stephen Davies*.

This book is also to deliver an ongoing legacy aimed at raising awareness of the impact Missionaries and Missions had in the South Seas, including Cape York and the Torres Strait, with a particular focus on the sailing ships involved in the trade and the communities, villages and Islands in which they operated.

The Last Mission Ship - Part One is the first of a three-part book series. Part Two will be in-depth history of Missionaries and their ships of the South Pacific and Part Three being the history, restoration and relaunch of the MV *Stephen Davies* itself.

The MV *Stephen Davies* is the last Missionary ship ever built to work under sail for Australian, New Guinea and South Pacific Missions.

MV *Stephen Davies* was built in Brisbane in 1951 for the Anglican Church's Cape York and Torres Strait mission agency, the *Australian Board of Missions* and named after the third Bishop of Carpentaria, the Right Reverend Stephen Davies.

The Last Mission Ship - Part One is aimed at gaining support for her future restoration and return to service. We hope readers can support our work through ongoing contributions, providing support through other means and sharing our story amongst your networks, your churches, your business contacts, community groups and schools.

There is opportunity for supporters of this initiative through monthly membership, giving exclusive access to videos, updates, merchandise and access to the completed book series once published, and also the opportunity to join the ship on one of her voyages throughout Cape York and the Torres Strait as a member.

We are also seeking more stories about Missions and Mission Ships in service in Australia, Papua, New Guinea and the South Seas. If you have information, photographs, stories or artefacts please get in touch.

We are hoping to return MV *Stephen Davies* to some level of service, particularly to her old sailing grounds throughout Cape York and the Torres Strait, and if possible, throughout Papua New Guinea. The Ship may be provided to various groups and churches for their own work and to community and educational institutions to bring her history to future generations.

We are not sure what form this future service looks like, however, the ship will certainly become a messenger for good, perhaps carrying cargo and people and creating new stories along the way.

Keep the *Faith*

FROM THE PEN OF
MICHAEL L SMITH
Uncharted Collective

Source: Chris De Vine

faith

PREFACE

Before time, the quest of the Missionaries was to bring Christianity to the Islands of the South Seas and challenge the dark practices of the so-called heathens and their warfare, sorcery and black magic, headhunting and cannibalism.

For centuries, these practices plagued Indigenous people in the South Pacific including the Australian mainland, Torres Strait, Papua, New Guinea, New Hebrides (Vanuatu) and the Solomon Islands.

Whilst the Missionaries did indeed, bring the "Light", they also forbid and suppressed many things including culture, language and traditions in the quest for Christianity and what was righteous in their view.

Therein lies the quest. The Missionaries were friend and foe, Government partner and their opposition, enabler and disabler.

Such was the circumstance of the Government's White Australia Policy, forced assimilation, stolen generations and blatant disregard for Aboriginal and Torres Strait Islander people for identity, rights and recognition, the Missionaries were dealt with a strange hand indeed.

MISSIONS OF THE SOUTH SEAS

Missionaries were present throughout the South Pacific and Australian waters, most notably with Tahiti in 1817 with the Reverend John Williams, New Caledonia in 1841, New Hebrides (Vanuatu) in 1846 and Papua and New Guinea in 1870. In Queensland, the first missionaries arrived at Somerset in 1867 in what became a failed attempt, followed shortly after by the Torres Strait in 1871.

Missionary Ship *John Williams*. Source: Public Domain

The Missionaries all had one thing in common... their need and concern with the sea. Their only chance to conduct Mission work was by sea and they needed sailing ships capable of doing the work.

This led to a significant increase in ship building, specifically for the purpose of church missions and outreach work throughout the South Pacific. These ships needed to carry passengers, cargo and materials through treacherous, uncharted waters, to an Island that may not be all that welcoming to the new visitors when they arrived.

The connection of Missionary work to colonialism in the South
Pacific is varied. Many missionaries were stout defenders of the
independence of their Missions, opponents of colonial expansion, the
Blackbirders and the resource raiders.

Others were willing partners with colonial administrations. For
example, establishing Missions to assist with regulating recruitment into
the Torres Strait pearling fleet. Some went a step further and owned
and operated their own Pearl Luggers for the 'benefit' of the Missions,
but not necessarily benefit any of the crew.

In the South Pacific and Australia there have been many missionary
ships of great interest and history. Ranging in size from 20 tons to
almost 700 tons, and 60 feet to more than 200 feet.

Many Mission Ships were named after their missionaries, from the
seven ships named after Missionary John Williams, to the many
Southern Cross ships, with others inspired by local language names. All
Mission Ships in the early days worked under sail, with many the typical
South Sea Schooner of 70 - 90 foot.

Melanesian Mission Ship **Southern Cross**, Source: Public Domain

Between the 1840s and the 1890s almost every island group in the Pacific was brought within one of the colonial empires including Britain, France, Spain, Dutch, Germany and the United States.

The South Pacific had been a stronghold for Missionaries, Traders, Resource Raiders and Blackbirders in the 1860's, particularly in New Caledonia and New Hebrides (Vanuatu).

Source: Blackbirding in the Pacific, Public Domain

The 1860's saw the French Government seeking the removal of Missionaries and other Traders from the Loyalty Islands and New Caledonia. This included the likes of Captain William Banner, known for his role in Blackbirding, trading and resource raiding, who was forced out of the region in 1859. He went on to start the pearl shelling era in the Torres Strait in 1868 with his own South Sea Islander crew, .

As with Captain Banner, the London Missionary Society were also forced to leave New Caledonia and the Loyalties, as ordered by the French Government in 1869. It was then that the LMS decided to expand, for the first time, into the Torres Strait and New Guinea.

THE FIRST CAPE YORK MISSION

The Colonial outpost of Somerset was established in 1864 by John Jardine who was appointed by the Government of Queensland as a magistrate in a new frontier region of British Colonisation. With the aid of a contingent of Royal Marines, John sailed there in August 1864.

The first Missionary in the Torres Strait or Cape York region was with Reverend F.C. Jagg, who was appointed on behalf of the *Society for the Propagation of Gospel in Foreign Parts,* and arrived in Somerset with his family on 15 March 1867 on board the small ship *HMS Salamander.* HMS *Salamander* was an 818 ton paddlewheel, three-masted sloop, under the command of Captain J. Carnegie.

HMS Salamander was a vital link for Somerset, bringing in supplies by sea, on average three times a year. As well as the Reverend F.C. Jagg, school teacher Mr. W.I. Kennett also came to Somerset and started a mission school on 1 October 1867. Both men were representatives of the England based Society and were charged with establishing a mission at Somerset.

HMs Salamanda

Source:
John Oxley Library,
Queensland

However, these early missionaries were unable to overcome the challenges they faced at Somerset. A lack of funding, lack of support from the Jardine's and the Government, and dismay at the brutality of the police, meant that the Somerset Mission was closed by June 1868.

Source: Jardine Vidgen Family Collection

John Jardine's son Frank was by this time now in charge of Somerset and the arrival of a Missionary Ship in 1872 changed the course of his life and his new bride. The Ship was carrying Sana Solia, a Samoan Princess and German educated niece of King Malietoa of Samoa.

Sana was a Missionary, on board a Mission Ship that was travelling from New Caledonia to New Guinea in an attempt to set up the first missions there for the *London Missionary Society*. The LMS had been to Erub the year before in what is known as Coming of the Light, and this time planned to push into New Guinea by picking up some Torres Strait Missionaries along the way.

Frank had been in Somerset as Government Resident and Magistrate since 1867. The LMS Missionaries and their ship stopped to replenish, provision and advise the Government Resident of their plans to go through the Torres Strait and onto New Guinea.

Frank took a liking to Sana, and against her wishes, and those of the Missionaries, wanted her to stay. Despite this, some stories state they did depart and Frank took his Cutter and sailed after the ship, boarded and convinced Sana to come with him, some say by the use of his position and some force.

However, in a true love story, Frank and Sana got married on 16th October 1873, had four children and lived together for 47 years until Frank died in 1919. She died four years later in 1923. Both are buried at Somerset.

Source: Jardine Vidgen Family Collection

THE TORRES STRAIT

Torres Strait is named after a Spanish captain, Luís Viez De Torres, who sailed through Torres Strait in 1606 on his way to Manila in the Philippines. He sailed along the south coast of New Guinea and mapped the strait that still bears his name.

He wrote a letter to the King of Spain describing his voyage, but was kept hidden from mapmakers until in 1769, when Scottish geographer Alexander Dalrymple found De Torres' notes proving a passage south of New Guinea. Alexander named the Torres Strait after De Torres.

Captain James Cook eventually led the British expedition to "find the Southern Land". In 1770 Cook landed on Bedanug (Possession Island), originally for an exercise to find a navigable passage through the Strait.

There were at least three re-writes of Cook's Journal, including significant differences between the original and the last. It is argued that whilst in Batavia, when Cook learnt that the French had preceded him across the Pacific, Cook may have re-wrote this "navigation" drill on Bedanug as a "possession ceremony" instead of the navigation exercise it was, and that he had claimed Australia's east coast for the British Crown.

It appears Cook, and the British Admiralty, may have claimed Australia from the far side of the world, in the numerous re-writes of Cook's Journal, long after the voyage. If this is the case, then as an afterthought to counter claims by the French landing in Australia first, Cook took possession of a country whilst he wasn't even there.

TORRES STRAIT MISSIONS

It was the 1st of July 1871, when the London Missionary Society (LMS) finally arrived in the Torres Strait on the Mission Ship *Surprise* after being forced to leave the Loyalty Islands and New Caledonia in 1869.

Reverend Samuel McFarlane and Reverend Archibald Murray, together with eight Loyalty Island mission teachers, arrived at Darnley Island (Erub) in the Torres Strait. That single event has come to be known as the *Coming of the Light* and which is now celebrated by Torres Strait Islanders annually.

Two missionaries stayed on Erub while the remaining missionaries travelled to Warrior Island (Tudu), where they were welcomed by none other than self-made Master Pearler, notable Blackbirder and resource raider, Captain William Banner, who had established a pearling station on the island the year before.

Loyalty Islander missionaries were then left at Saibai, Dauan, Yorke and Yam Islands, while Mission Ship *Surprise* sailed down to the newly established settlement at Somerset.

The LMS established a temporary base there from where they could expand into other Torres Strait Islands and the mainland of New Guinea, having been their focus all along.

Between 1871 and 1878 more than 130 South Sea Islander teachers, mainly from Loyalty Islands, Cook Islands, Niue, Society Islands and Rurutu, taught in the Torres Strait and New Guinea, along with their wives and families. This included Princess Sana Solina in 1872 who was voyaging from New Caledonia to New Guinea when, having stopped at Somerset on their way, became Somerset's Keeper after marrying Government Resident and Magistrate Frank Jardine.

From that time in 1871 the London Missionary Society worked among the islands of the Torres Strait until just prior to World War I in 1914.

Source: Coming of the Light, LMS

In 1908 the Government Resident based on Thursday Island officially *faith* approached the Anglican Bishop on Thursday Island, Bishop Gilbert White, to take over some missionary work in the Torres Strait, specifically the community at St Paul's Village on Mua (Moa) that was yet to be involved with the London Missionary Society.

The Anglican Church had been working throughout Cape York but had stopped short of competing with the LMS in the Torres Strait. Bishop White apparently confessed to wanting the Islands but stood clear until asked by the Government. Supported by the LMS, The Anglican Church was able to establish a mission on St Pauls for the recently established South Sea Islander community. The Anglican Church and their agency the Australian Board of Missions was now firmly entrenched in Cape York and the Torres Strait.

The Mission at St Pauls was a little different to the root. They were not Torres Strait Islanders but South Sea Islanders who had come to settle there as a result of pearling, sugar plantations and the White Australia Policy's attempt in removing these recruits from the country.

The first South Sea Islanders who settled at St Pauls were the Ware family who were originally based on Maubiag, but had issues with the families there over a marriage proposal, and sought refuge on the deserted village of Wug (now St Pauls) in 1903.

This was the first South Sea Islander village established in the Torres Strait. Once it was known that a Wug Traditional Owner had invited South Sea Islanders to settle there, many others came.

Captain William Bligh, in charge of the British Navy ships Providence and Assistant, visited the Torres Strait in 1792 and named Moa 'Banks Island' in honour of the botanist Sir Joseph Banks.

Deaconess Florence Buchanan assumed responsibility for the fundamentalist non-denominational South Seas Evangelical Mission (also known as the Queensland Kanaka Mission).

Despite an accident in 1888 where she almost lost a foot, as an act of thanks to God she desired to take the vows of "Deaconess," and on January 5, 1908, while a torrential storm of rain raged outside the Cathedral, a beautiful peace reigned within, while Bishop White ordained Florence Griffiths Buchanan to be first Deaconess in the Diocese of Carpentaria.

It was during the months following that the need for a teacher at Moa became urgent; with characteristic humility and the ever-present desire to give others the first chance, she waited, until, no one offering, she said "Here am I, send me." In 1908, Florence sailed to Moa from Thursday Island to take up as the Pioneer Missionary and teacher.

VENTURERS
FOR GOD

FLORENCE
BUCHANAN

REVEREND STEPHEN DAVIES

Saturday, 17th December 1921 in Queensland newspapers -

"Officially announced that Reverend Stephen Harris Davies, lately head of the Charleville Brotherhood, has accepted the Bishopric of Carpentaria, which was offered to him recently by the Bishops of the province of Queensland.

The new Bishop is expected to reach Queensland some time in March, when arrangements for his enthronement will take place. It will be remembered that when a vacancy in the Bishopric ot New Guinea was created by the resignation of Archbishop Sharp it was filled by the appointment of the Reverend Dr. Newton, Bishop of Carpentaria, who is to be enthroned Bishop of New Guinea early in the new year.

The appointment of Mr. Davies as Archbishop of Carpentaria is regarded as another recognition of the missionary works of the Anglican Church. Mr Davies was educated for the ministry at the clergy college at Leeds, England.

He proceeded to Emanuel College, Cambridge, where he graduated in 1905, and was ordained deacon by the Bishop of Ripon in 1909, when he was appointed curate at St Matthew's, Hollbeck.

He was ordained priest in 1911, and in 1912 he came to Queensland and joined the Charleville Brotherhood, with whom he remained until 1920, having served for some years as head of that organisation."

A BISHOP ENTHRONED

Reverend Stephen Davies, was enthroned at Thursday Island, as third Bishop of Carpentaria on 23rd April 1922. It was noted at the time by the Church that he had come to the Carpentaria Diocese with a *"practical knowledge of the bush, an essential qualification for the Bishop of the largest diocese (in area) in Australia. He is young, and so retains the vigour so necessary for his arduous journeys."*

At the enthronement service, two Islander clergy, Reverend Joseph Lui and Reverend Poey Passi, both of whom are Torres Strait islanders working in the Torres Strait Mission, were present.

Bishop Davies was forced to leave Thursday Island for more than four years during the war with Japanese bombings in Darwin and the Torres Strait. World War II had major implications for some of the Carpentaria Diocese both in the Northern Territory and on Thursday Island.

In once instance in 1939, the Naval authorities in Darwin resumed the Anglican Church for Defence purposes to convert the building into a naval drill hall. The local papers reported that:

"The Right Rev. Stephen Davies, Bishop of Carpentaria, threatened today to demolish his own Church because the naval authorities proposed converting it into a naval drill hall."

After the war ended, Bishop Davies returned to the Torres Strait in 1946 to begin the difficult task of re-establishing the diocese.

After 27 long years, the Bishop was forced to retire due to illness and left the Islands and returned to Brisbane in August and officially ceased duty on 30th September 1949.

The diocese is bounded by the Queensland coast and Northern Territory coast on the east and north, the Northern Territory and the Queensland boundary on the west, and thence easterly and north-easterly by a line covering the Northern Territory boundary and much of Queensland, and from a point in the far west nearly opposite Brisbane by an irregular course to Cape Bedford, in the north.

It embraces the whole of the Northern Territory. The area is 620,000 square miles, and the scattered population consists of 10,000 whites, 5000 Japanese, Chinese, and other aliens, and 35,000 aborigines.

The *See* town (Latin for *sedes*, meaning 'seat') is Thursday Island where the Bishop is based. The Jurisdiction extends through the islands of the Strait and the Coral Sea. Among the centres served are Alice Springs and Tennant Creek.

Source: Editorial Committee of the Centenary Celebrations, Melboune Diocese, 1947

THE LAST MISSION SHIPS

faith

Two of the last Mission ships were built in Queensland by Norman Wright and Sons for the *Australian Board of Missions,* including the MV *Torres Herald* in 1938 and the last being MV *Stephen Davies* in 1951.

MISSION VESSEL TORRES HERALD

MISSION VESSEL STEPHEN DAVIES

MISSION SHIP STEPHEN DAVIES

The Missionary Vessel (MV) *Stephen Davies* was built in Brisbane in 1951 for the Anglican Church's mission agency, the *Australian Board of Missions* and named after the third Bishop of Carpentaria, Stephen Davies who took office in 1922.

  MV *Stephen Davies* is most likely the last Mission Vessel ever built to operate under sail that we are aware of for Australian, New Guinea and South Pacific Missions. MV *Stephen Davies* was built as an auxiliary ketch, gaff rigged with main and mizzen mast, steered by tiller, and voyaged between church-led missions on Western and Eastern Cape York and St Pauls village on Moa in the Torres Strait.

Dedicated by Archbishop

faith

DEDICATION ceremony being performed by Archbishop Halse on board the new mission ketch Stephen Davies at Bulimba yesterday.

Set to sail for mission

Ten Torres Strait islanders sang native hymns yesterday at the naming and dedication ceremony of the Australian Board of Mission launch Stephen Davies.

The launch is named after The Rt. Rev. Stephen Davies, Bishop of Carpentaria for 25 years, now living in retirement. Mrs. Davies officially named the launch.

The Rev. Kabay Pilot, a Torres Strait Islander and assistant priest of All Souls Cathedral, Thursday Island, assisted Archbishop Halse in the dedication ceremony.

A St. George flag, a gift from the Comrades of St. George was broken out at the masthead. This is the flag under which the launch will sail.

Source: THE COURIER MAIL, 5th May 1951

She continued service to Cape York and the Torres Strait when the
Department of Native Affairs, later known as the Department of
Aboriginal and Islander Affairs, took over the missions from the Church
in 1967, and in doing so, took over ownership of MV *Stephen Davies*.

Some referred to her as the *"Gulf Liner"*, now a cargo boat, registered
to carry 20 ton of cargo from Thursday Island to the communities
throughout Cape York and the Torres Strait up until the mid 1980's for
the Department who ran the community stores.

DNA/DAIA trucks would deliver supplies for building, medical aid posts
and schools to the wharf where they were loaded onto the boat. The
Island Industries Board (IIB) would arrange for food stuffs to be loaded
for their stores. During it's time with the DAIA and IIB, the mizzen (aft)
mast was removed to assist with better cargo loading capacity and
ability. Reverting more to motor rather than sail, she was powered by a
Rolls Royce engine, and did exceptional speeds between Islands.

In the 1980's, the Department of Aboriginal and Islander Affairs put MV *Stephen Davies* out to tender with the successful bidder being Ray Cousins who became the first private individual to take over ownership.

From 1990 until 2002 it was owned by Shipwright Steve Thornally and his wife Sue Gould who is a descendant of the Karaureg people. From 2002 until 2019 it was owned by Mike and Debbie Rawlings from the Sunshine Coast.

MV *Stephen Davies* was taken over by the Saltwater Club in 2019 and had her restoration commenced until COVID forced the halt of all operations at that time.

Source: Norman Chris De Vine

PEARL LUGGER HERITAGE FLEET

faith

The *Pearl Lugger Heritage Fleet* was established in 2013 and was an ambitious campaign to preserve & promote maritime history and culture of Cape York, Torres Strait and the South Seas.

There are only a dozen Torres Strait pearl luggers remaining, of which the Fleet was the custodians of three including *Antonia* A99, *Anniki* A98 and *Triton* A82. There are only two Mission Ships remaining, with MV *Stephen Davies* acquired in 2019.

There is no call for Mission Ships of old, Blackbirding ships are long gone, and the elders and ancestors stories are in danger of being lost and forgotten.

Now is the time to invest in the future, and this can only be done by enabling us to preserve the past! But your help is needed with these vessels, ensuring the history and traditions of Northern Australia's maritime cultural heritage continues to be saved.

These ships need a new mission - a new purpose - and that will be youth sail training, education and events. MV *Stephen Davies* could serve as a multi-use vessel including a voyaging maritime museum, leadership programs, education and youth activities and cultural events and festival attendance such as *Coming of the Light* celebrations throughout Queensland.

The ships can also provide a unique cultural tourism experience of the maritime history and traditions including pearling, Beche-de-Mer, missionaries, Blackbirding, WWII, trading links, first encounters with Captain Cook and more.

Former crew of pearl luggers and the mission boats would visit the ship *faith* including Uncle George Mosby who also makes all of our models including one of MV *Stephen Davies*.